MOTORSPORTS

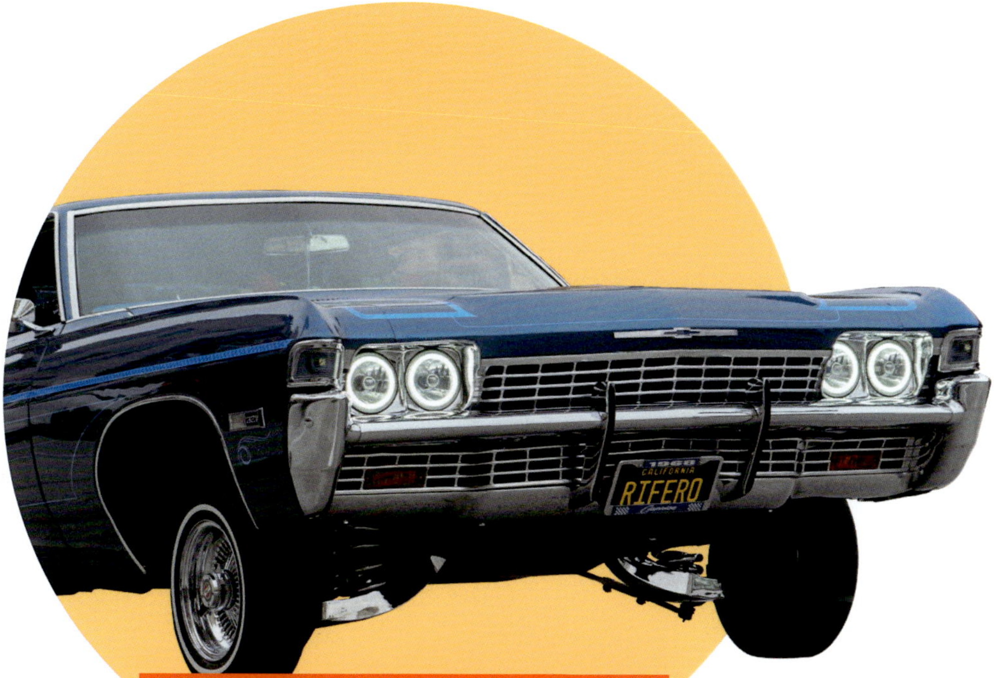

LOWRIDERS

by Alissa Thielges

body

paint job

Look for these words and pictures as you read.

tire

car show

A lowrider is a sweet ride.
Look at it go!

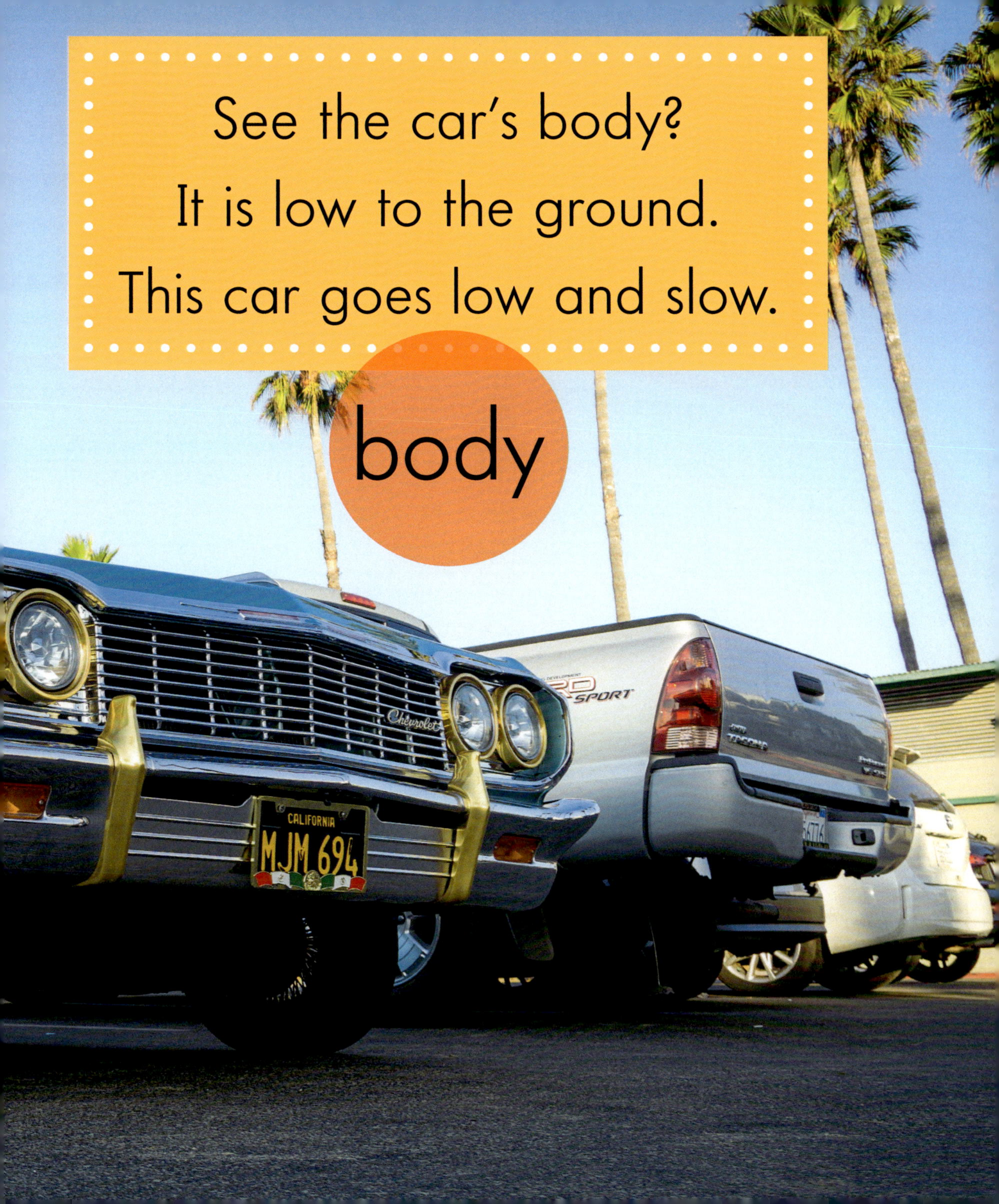
See the car's body?
It is low to the ground.
This car goes low and slow.

body

See the paint job?

Drivers use paint to tell a story.

Each car is a work of art.

paint job

OR SHOW

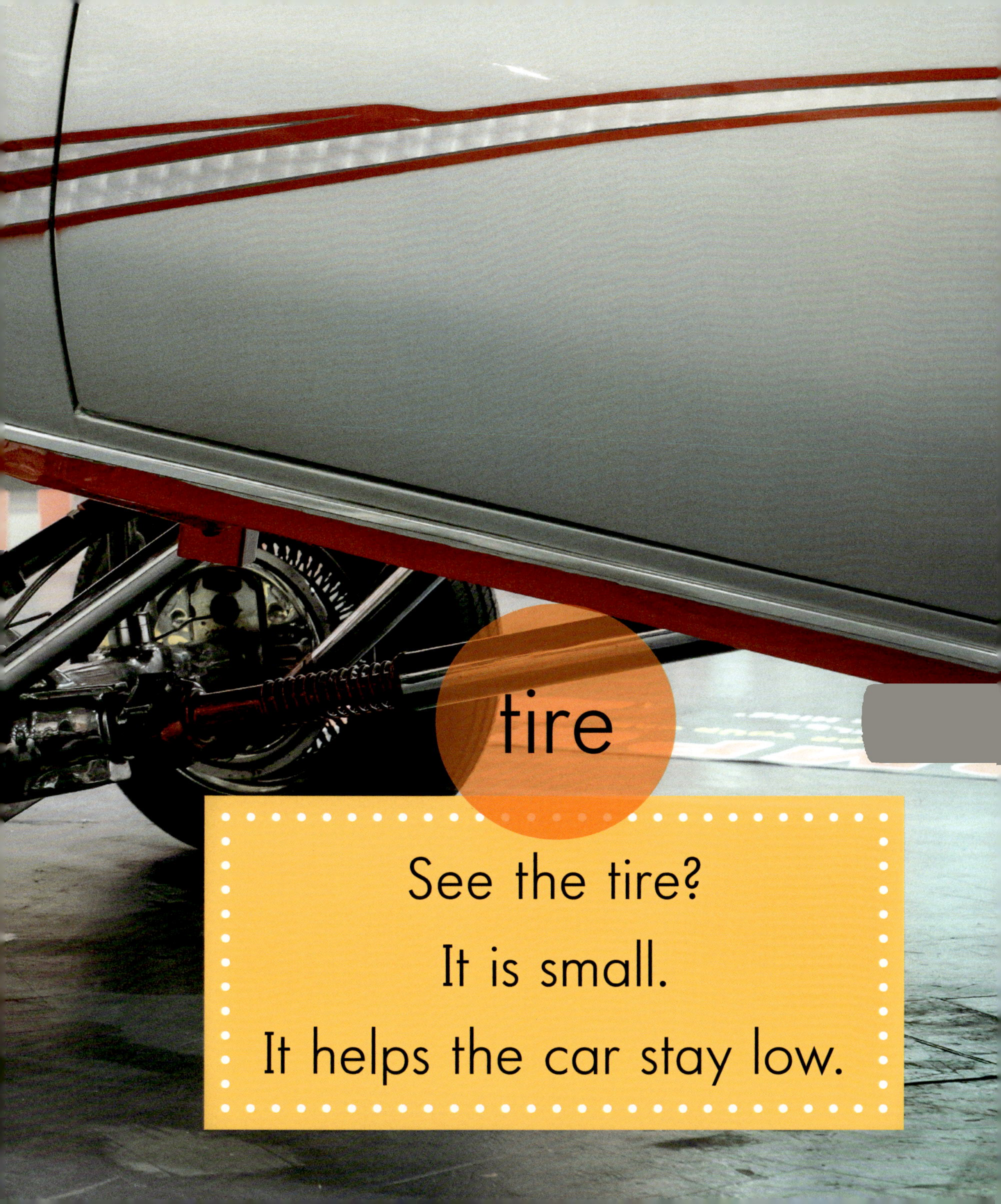

tire

See the tire?
It is small.
It helps the car stay low.

See the car hopping?
The tire comes off the ground.
It looks like the car is dancing.

NO
TRESPASSING
NO LOITERING
OR
CONGREGATING
CALIFORNIA
SIX4LOW
ELLIS BROOKS
Chevrolet

See the car show?
Drivers see who can
hop the highest.
They can win a prize.
car show

A lowrider joins a parade.
It hops as it drives. How fun!

body

paint job

Did you find?

tire

car show

Spot is published by Amicus Learning, an imprint of Amicus
P.O. Box 227, Mankato, MN 56002
www.amicuspublishing.us

Library of Congress Cataloging-in-Publication Data
Names: Thielges, Alissa, 1995- author.
Title: Lowriders / by Alissa Thielges.
Description: Mankato, MN : Amicus Learning, [2026] |
    Series: Spot motorsports | Audience: Ages 4-7 |
    Audience: Grades K-1 | Summary: "Lowriders
    are slow-moving cars with custom paint jobs and
    very low bodies. They hop along the road in
    parades and car shows. This search-and-find book
    reinforces new vocabulary words with simple facts
    and compelling photographs to teach kindergarten
    readers about motorsports"— Provided by publisher.
Identifiers: LCCN 2024050079 (print) | LCCN 2024050080
    (ebook) | ISBN 9798892004848 (library binding) |
    ISBN 9798892005388 (paperback) |
    ISBN 9798892005920 (ebook)
Subjects: LCSH: Lowriders—Juvenile literature. |
    Automobiles—Customizing—Juvenile literature. |
    CYAC: Lowriders. | Automobiles.
Classification: LCC TL255.2 .T54 2026 (print) | LCC TL255.2
    (ebook) | DDC 629.222—dc23/eng/20241219
LC record available at https://lccn.loc.gov/2024050079
LC ebook record available at https://lccn.loc.
    gov/2024050080

Ana Brauer, editor
Deb Miner, series designer
Sara Hood, book designer
 and photo researcher